P9-BZI-243

The Life and Times of

George Frideric Handel

P.O. Box 196
Hockessin, Delaware 19707

Titles in the Series

The Life and Times of...

Johann Sebastian Bach
Ludwig van Beethoven
Irving Berlin
Hector Berlioz
Leonard Bernstein
Johannes Brahms
Frederic Chopin
Duke Ellington
Stephen Foster
Kenny G.
George Gershwin
George Frideric Handel
Franz Joseph Haydn
Scott Joplin
Franz Liszt
Felix Mendelssohn
Wolfgang Amadeus Mozart
Franz Peter Schubert
John Philip Sousa
Igor Stravinsky
Peter Ilyich Tchaikovsky
Giuseppe Verdi
Antonio Lucio Vivaldi
Richard Wagner

The Life and Times of

George Frideric Handel

by Jim Whiting

Printing 1 2 3 4 5 6 7 8

Library of Congress Cataloging-in-Publication Data

Whiting, Jim, 1943-

The Life and Times of George Frideric Handel/Jim Whiting.

p. cm. — (Masters of music. The world's greatest composers)

Summary: Discusses the life and career of the eighteenth-century German composer. Includes bibliographical references (p.) and index.

ISBN 1-58415-192-7 (lib bdg.)

1. Handel, George Frideric, 1685-1759—Juvenile literature. 2. Composers—Biography—Juvenile literature. [1. Handel, George Frideric, 1685-1759. 2. Composers. I. Title. II. Series.

ML3930.H25 W58 2003

780'.92—dc21 2002153347

ABOUT THE AUTHOR: Jim Whiting has been a journalist, writer, editor, and photographer for more than 20 years. In addition to a lengthy stint as publisher of *Northwest Runner* magazine, Mr. Whiting has contributed articles to the *Seattle Times*, *Conde Nast Traveler*, *Newsday*, and *Saturday Evening Post*. He has edited more than 60 titles in the Mitchell Lane Real-Life Reader Biography series and Unlocking the Secrets of Science. He is the author of numerous books for young adults, including *Charles Schulz* and *The Life and Times of Johann Sebastian Bach* (Mitchell Lane). His love of classical music inspired him to write this book. He lives in Washington state with his wife and two teenage sons.

PHOTO CREDITS: Cover: Photo Researchers; p. 6 Photo Researchers; p. 9 Corbis; p. 12 North Wind Picture Archives; p. 14 SuperStock; p. 16 Stephanie Kondrchek; p. 18 Christie's Images/Corbis; p. 19 Archivo Iconografico, SA/Corbis; p. 20 Corbis; p. 22 National Portrait Gallery, London; p. 24 Corbis; p. 26 Photo Researchers; p. 29 Corbis; p. 32 Angelo Hornak/Corbis; p. 38 John Garrett/Corbis

PUBLISHER'S NOTE: This story is based on the author's extensive research, which he believes to be accurate. Documentation of such research is contained on page 46.

The internet sites referenced herein were active as of the publication date. Due to the fleeting nature of some Web sites, we cannot guarantee they will all be active when you are reading this book.

Contents

The Life and Times of

George Frideric Handel

by Jim Whiting

* For Your Information

This portrait of Handel was painted sometime during the 1720s, so he would have been in his late 30s or early 40s. It is less formal than most portraits, because Handel is shown in his ordinary clothing and he isn't wearing a wig. The artist is the French painter Phillippe Mercier. Mercier was born in 1689 and died in 1760, so he is almost an exact contemporary of Handel.

Swords Unsheathed

There was no way out. His army had been soundly defeated, his enemies were closing in. Completely surrounded, he had no chance of escaping. He knew that if he were captured, he would be led in chains in front of the jeering population. For a man as proud as he was, that thought could not be tolerated. The humiliation would be too great. And afterward, he would probably be executed anyway. Maybe he would even be tortured first. It would be too dangerous for his enemies to let such a famous man stay alive.

He shook his head sadly. There was only one thing to do.

He pulled his sword, stabbed himself in the stomach, and slowly collapsed.

The applause was thunderous.

Smiling, the man quickly jumped back to his feet and bowed to the audience. He was Johann Mattheson, a twenty-two-year-old German opera singer. He had just performed the role of Mark Antony, a famous Roman general. But he wasn't just a performer. He had also composed this opera, *Cleopatra.* Despite his youth, it was already his third opera. He was a famous man.

Within an hour he would draw his sword again. But this time it wouldn't be on a stage. It would be in front of the theater in Hamburg, Germany, where *Cleopatra* had just been performed. And he wouldn't be acting. He would be trying to kill someone. For real.

His opponent was nineteen-year-old George Frideric Handel.

During the opera, Handel had been playing the harpsichord, an instrument similar to a piano, in the orchestra pit. Orchestras at that time didn't have a conductor, as they do today, standing in front of everyone with a baton. The harpsichordist was the leader of the orchestra.

As the applause from the suicide scene died down, Mattheson walked briskly across the stage and down into the orchestra pit. His role was done, but the opera would not be over for another half hour. According to the custom of the times, he would take over the harpsichord for that final half hour. After all, he was the composer. He believed that he knew better than anyone else how the music should be played. Handel was supposed to get up and join the violin section.

For some reason, Handel refused to move. With hundreds of spectators and performers looking on, the two young men—who had been good friends for more than a year—started shouting. Then they shoved each other. Much later in life, Mattheson wrote, "Handel, at the time of the quarrel, was tall, strong, broad-shouldered, and muscular," so the scuffle was probably similar to a fight in a football locker room.

Somehow they finished the show, but both men were still very angry. Several members of the orchestra egged them on. As they arrived at the stage door, Mattheson slapped Handel across the face.

London's New Covent Garden Theatre, shown here, was the scene of many performances of Handel's operas between 1734 and 1737. The huge stage sloped downward toward the audience. The three tiers of boxes on each side were used by the nobility and the upper classes. Above them are two more tiers, called "slips." All five levels were elaborately decorated. The main floor held the gallery, the location of the least expensive seating. Much of it consisted of backless benches. Lighting came from candles in the chandeliers and torches that were fastened to the walls. These may have been the cause of a fire that burned down the theater in 1808. It was quickly rebuilt and reopened the following year.

Surrounded by so many people, Handel couldn't back down. He stepped into the street and drew his sword. Mattheson did the same thing. They circled each other warily, waving their swords back and forth. A couple of times they thrust toward each other, but the attacks were quickly parried.

Suddenly Mattheson saw his chance. He lunged forward, the tip of his sword pointed directly at Handel's heart.

Because it was early December and chilly outside, both men were wearing heavy coats. Their coats had large ornate brass buttons down the front. Mattheson's blade struck one of Handel's buttons. The blade glanced off and shattered.

The close call brought the two young men to their senses. They were still very angry, but they realized that they didn't seriously want to kill each other. They stalked away.

A few weeks later some mutual friends brought Mattheson and Handel together. The two men shook hands and made up.

Mattheson concluded, "I had the honor of entertaining Handel to dinner after which we went to the rehearsal of his *Almira* [an opera that Handel had just finished writing] and became better friends than before."

Thirty-seven years after the duel, Handel wrote *Messiah,* perhaps the most famous piece of music ever composed. Every year during the Christmas season, millions of people attend live performances of *Messiah.* Millions more listen to it on recordings. The Hallelujah chorus from *Messiah* is so revered that people stand up while it is being sung. That chorus is so well known that it is often used in movies and advertisements.

If it hadn't been for that big brass button, Handel would never have lived to compose it.

BARBER-SURGEONS

FYInfo

Today it would be unthinkable for someone to be both a professional barber and a surgeon. But before and during Handel's time, the combination was actually very common. The practice began during the Middle Ages. Originally, clergymen were responsible for performing surgeries—until the Pope decreed that priests could no longer be responsible for shedding blood. Because barbers were familiar with the use of razors, it seemed logical for them to take over any function that involved the cutting of skin. Most doctors did not want to perform surgery as they thought it was a menial task.

Since the time of the ancient Greeks, around 400–600 B.C., it had been believed that the human body consisted of four humors, or liquids: blood, phlegm, yellow bile, and black bile. In a healthy person, the four humors would all be in balance. Illness resulted when there was an excess of one of the humors. The cure, therefore, was to reduce the amount of that humor.

By far the most common treatment was bleeding. It would be done either by making a deliberate cut in the person and letting some blood flow into a bowl, or by putting leeches—a type of bloodsucking worm—on the person's body. Bleeding was used to treat many different diseases, such as the flu, coughing, headaches, and even heart disease. Sometimes it was used as a preventive measure, like taking vitamins today.

The patient would often cling tightly to a pole to encourage the blood to flow. Afterward, the wound would be wrapped with a cloth. When it wasn't being used, the cloth—often still stained with blood—would be wrapped around the pole. Then it would be placed outside the barber's place of business as a primitive form of advertising. This is the origin of the modern barber's pole, which consists of alternating spirals of red and white.

Barber-surgeons didn't limit their practice to bleeding. They also performed other health-related functions such as pulling teeth, stitching wounds, and even amputations.

Today, thanks to anesthetics and vast improvements in sanitary conditions, operations are much safer than they were in Handel's time. People no longer think that surgery is a menial task. Surgeons are among the most highly trained members of the medical profession. Now we go to barbers to get our hair cut. We don't expect them to cut anything else.

A formal portrait of Handel by Jager. The long wig and elaborate apparel provide a contrast with the painting on page 6. Not all artists were as kind. In 1754, Joseph Goupy, Handel's stage manager, drew a side view of Handel playing the harpsichord. Called "The Charming Brute," it portrayed Handel as grossly overweight, with a pig's snout sticking out in front of his wig. Handel was insulted and cut Goupy out of his will.

The Making of a Musician

Georg Friedrich Händel (the original German spelling of his name) was born on February 23, 1685, in Halle. Halle is a large town in the province of Saxony, located in the northeastern portion of modern-day Germany.

His father was a successful barber-surgeon who was also named Georg Händel. At the time of his son's birth, he was sixty-three. His first wife had died in 1682. Following the custom of the times, he remarried within a few months. His new wife was Dorothea Taust, the daughter of a pastor. She was twenty-nine years younger than her husband. The couple's first child, a boy, lived for only an hour. Georg Friedrich, the second son, would soon be joined by two sisters.

By chance, another famous composer, Johann Sebastian Bach, was born less than a month after Handel. His birthplace was the town of Eisenach, about seventy-five miles from Halle. Even though they grew up so close together, the two would never meet.

Bach and Handel, who eventually changed the spelling of his name to George Frideric Handel, became the most famous composers of what is today called Baroque music. It is characterized by

the use of complex forms, a great deal of ornamentation, and combining contrasting elements (such as loud and soft tones) to create a sense of drama.

There was one major difference between Bach and Handel. Bach came from a family that had produced musicians for several generations. At a young age, his parents encouraged him to learn how to play several instruments. There was nothing in Handel's background to suggest that he would become a musician. His grandfather was a coppersmith, and his much older half brothers became doctors. His uncles on his mother's side were clergymen.

While we don't know much about Handel's childhood, he probably began school at about the age of six or seven. It appears that he began playing music at about the same time. That's not surpris-

Johann Sebastian Bach was born a month after Handel. Unlike Handel, he came from a family that could trace its musical background for several generations. Bach was more famous during his lifetime as an organist than a composer. By the time of his death in 1750 his works were regarded as old-fashioned. Four of his sons became composers, and their music became more popular than their father's. Today, however, many people consider Bach to be the greatest composer of all time.

ing, because many German towns during that time put a lot of importance on music. They hired organists whose salary was paid for by the town. In addition, many noblemen paid musicians to live at their courts and play regular concerts for them and their guests.

The youngster's interest in music caused an almost immediate conflict. Handel's father, not unreasonably, wanted his son to choose a career in which he could make a good living. He wanted him to become a lawyer. He thought that music was a waste of time and energy. He discouraged his son's efforts to learn how to play music. He may even have forbidden him to play.

But young Georg was determined. According to one story, he snuck a tiny clavichord, a keyboard instrument similar to the modern-day piano, into the house. He practiced late at night when everyone else was asleep.

All his hard work paid off a few years later.

His older half brother Karl worked at the nearby court of Johann Adolf, Duke of Saxe-Weissenfels. One day the senior Georg brought young Georg along to pay Karl a visit.

During their stay, young Georg was playing an organ. The duke heard him and was very impressed. He told the father that his son should have every opportunity to develop his talent. His father respectfully disagreed, but he didn't have much choice. It was not a good idea to oppose the will of a nobleman.

As a result, when they returned home, the boy began taking formal lessons. He was fortunate that one of the very best music teachers in Germany lived in Halle. His name was Friedrich Zachow, and he gave his young pupil a solid musical education. Handel learned how to play several instruments, including the harpsichord, organ, and violin. He also began to compose his own music.

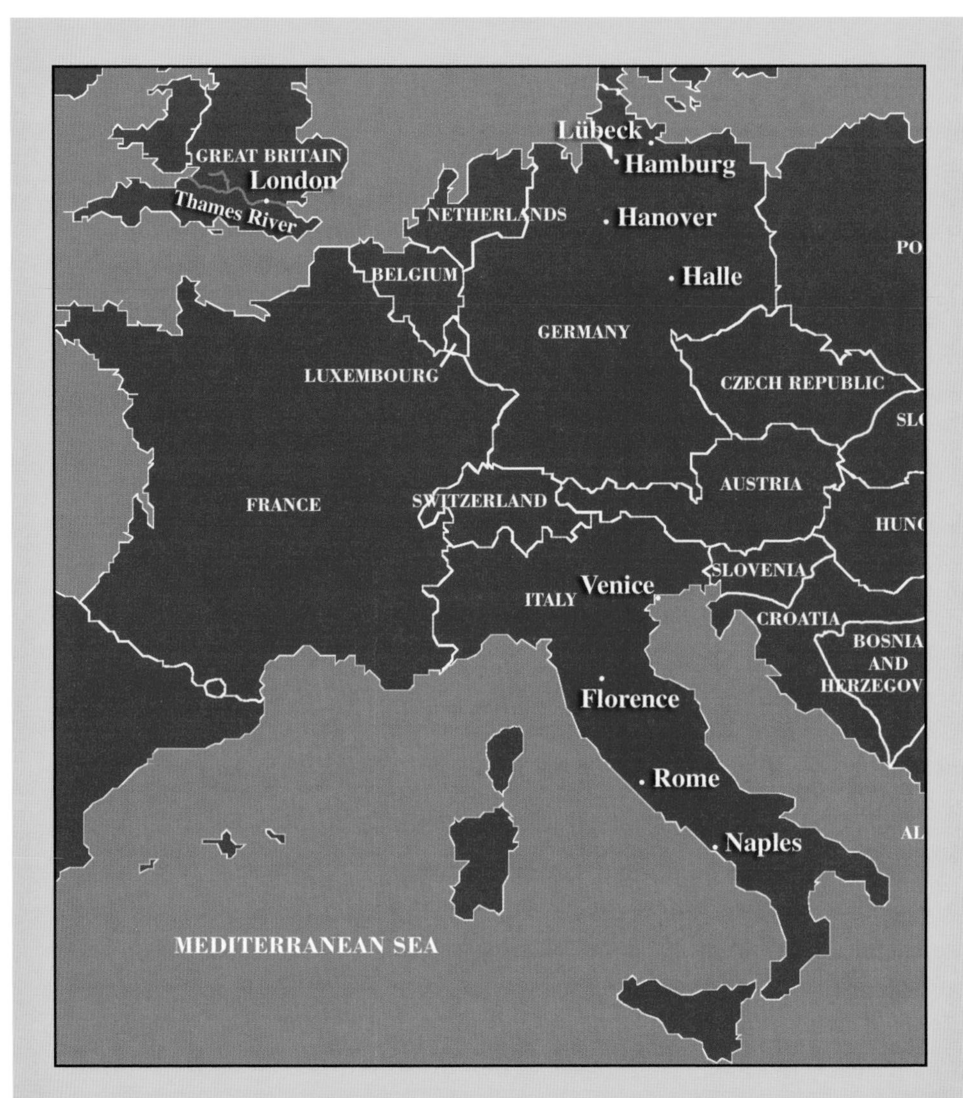

Map of Germany, Italy, and Great Britain that shows the locations of the cities that were important in Handel's career. His birthplace was Halle in Germany, he lived for several years in Italy as a young man, and he spent the largest part of his life in London. In 1727 he became a naturalized British citizen.

Handel's father died not long afterward, in early 1697. Young Georg became head of the household at the age of twelve. Five years later, he enrolled at the University of Halle. Respecting his father's wishes, he may have signed up to study law. But within a month, a church organist in Halle was fired. Handel was offered the job.

When his contract was finished a year later, he journeyed to Hamburg. The city had one of the most thriving music scenes in Germany at that time. It had a lot more to offer an ambitious young musician than the much smaller Halle.

Almost immediately after his arrival he met Mattheson, and the two young men became fast friends. So fast, in fact, that five weeks later they traveled together to the neighboring town of Lübeck. The organist there, Dietrich Buxtehude, wanted to retire. Handel and Mattheson may have considered replacing him.

The job, however, came with a tough string attached. Whoever took the position would have to marry Buxtehude's daughter Margreta. She was in her late twenties, an age at which women would long since have taken a husband. Neither of the men had any interest in marrying her, so they returned to Hamburg.

Johann Sebastian Bach would make a similar journey two years later and come to the same conclusion. Finally someone did take the position. At last Margreta had her husband.

In the meantime, Handel's career was starting to take off. In early 1705, a few weeks after the duel, his opera *Almira* premiered. With the popular Mattheson singing the lead role, it was a huge success.

His second opera, *Nero,* didn't do as well. He scraped together enough money to live on by playing in the orchestra and serving as a music teacher, but neither job was satisfactory.

This painting of Venice clearly shows its unique nature. In place of roads, hundreds of canals criss-cross the city. In Handel's time, people used gondolas and rowboats to get around. Today, nearly everyone uses powerboats. But tourists still enjoy a gondola ride. The artist is Canaletto (1697-1768), who made hundreds of drawings and paintings of Venice.

In 1706 he departed for Italy, a long and difficult journey over primitive roads. He believed he would have better opportunities there. Italian operas were becoming very popular all over Europe. They featured challenging arias for the singers that demonstrated their full vocal range, spectacular scenery, and plots based on ancient historical subjects that were familiar to the audience. In addition, everything—including the dialogue—was sung. The world's most famous singers were all Italians. The trip gave Handel an opportunity to learn about Italian opera firsthand. During the following few years, he would live in Florence, Naples, Rome, and Venice and compose a great deal of music.

He had another duel in Italy, probably in 1709, but this one didn't involve swords. It involved musical instruments. A nobleman organized a contest between Handel and the Italian composer Domenico Scarlatti, who was also born in 1685. Both would play the harpsichord and the organ to see which man was better on each one. The harpsichord contest was ruled a draw, but even Scarlatti agreed that Handel was a much better organ player.

This is a painting of the Italian composer Domenico Scarlatti, who like Handel and Bach was born in 1685. He came from a musical family and spent his entire career as a composer and keyboard player. He lived in Italy for his first 32 years, then moved to Portugal and Spain. He wrote seven operas and a great deal of sacred and secular vocal music. He is most famous for composing hundreds of keyboard sonatas. Scarlatti died in 1757.

This painting is entitled "View of Rome." It was painted in the early eighteenth century by Gaspar van Wittel, a Dutch painter who lived between 1653 and 1736. Handel lived in Rome for a brief period while he was a young man.

Also in 1709, Handel wrote an opera called *Agrippina* that was very successful and added to his growing reputation. His career was definitely on the upswing.

There were rumors that he was romantically involved with a singer during this time. Even if the rumors were true, nothing came of the courtship. Handel was destined to remain a bachelor. Though he was very famous during his lifetime, he was extremely secretive about his personal life, so we don't know why he never married.

There was certainly nothing wrong with him physically. Much later, the English King George III wrote, "Handel was very well built and lacked nothing in manliness." He added, "His amours [love affairs] were rather of short duration, always within the pale of his own profession."

Writing in 1799, a man named William Coxe said that Handel had had two opportunities to get married as a young man. The first ended when the young lady's mother said that she would never consent to her daughter's marrying a "fiddler," which stung Handel's pride. The other woman demanded that Handel give up music. There was no chance that that would happen.

With his years in Italy adding to his stature, Handel had no trouble getting a job in Germany when he returned in 1710. He took a position as kapellmeister (orchestra leader) at the court of Georg Ludwig, the elector (or ruler) of the province of Hanover. A few months later, he took a leave of absence to travel to England. Italian opera was just starting to become very popular there. Handel created an immediate sensation when he composed *Rinaldo.*

Soon afterward he returned to Hanover. It quickly became apparent that Hanover was not where he wanted to be. He longed to go back to England, and he began learning English.

It wasn't surprising that Handel liked England so much. The influence of Parliament made the country more democratic than Germany was. Because Handel spent so much time there, his development was very different from Bach's. Back in Germany, Bach went through a succession of jobs, either being employed directly by a town or playing in the court of a nobleman. He was always on a fixed income. Sometimes he had problems making ends meet.

Handel, on the other hand, was very much his own man. He had the potential for making a great deal more money than Bach would

ever see. Or he could make nothing. There were no guarantees. Young and self-confident, Handel was willing to chance it.

He worked out an opportunity to take another trip there, but the elector, his employer, imposed one condition: He couldn't stay. He had to come back to Hanover "within a reasonable time."

Queen Anne of England (born in 1665 and became queen in 1702). This painting comes from the Studio of John Closterman and hangs in the National Portrait Gallery in London.

His second stint in England was even more successful. He wrote music that quickly became very popular, including a birthday composition for Queen Anne. She liked it so much that she awarded him a large yearly pension.

By then he had been gone from Hanover well beyond any reasonable expectation. The elector was angry with him.

Soon afterward, Queen Anne died.

Her successor was that same elector of Hanover. Now he was King George I of England. Suddenly Handel's future as a composer in England appeared to be in doubt.

REAL-LIFE ROBINSON CRUSOE

FYInfo

In 1719, English author Daniel Defoe published *Robinson Crusoe.* The novel is about a man who is the only survivor of a shipwreck. He lives alone on an uninhabited island in the Caribbean Sea for twenty-four years. He uses his ingenuity to solve the problems of day-to-day living. Reading the Bible brings him mental comfort. Eventually he saves a native from cannibals and names him Friday. Finally the two men capture a ship and return to England. It was one of the best-selling books of its time, and many people still read it today.

Defoe didn't make up his story out of thin air. He actually had a model, a man named Alexander Selkirk. Selkirk, born in Scotland in 1676, ran away to sea at the age of nineteen and soon became an excellent sailor. He was promoted to sailing master of a ship called the *Cinque Ports,* second only to the captain in importance.

On one occasion he disagreed with the captain, believing that the ship was in danger of sinking. In September 1704 he asked to be put ashore on a remote, uninhabited island called Juan Fernández. It lies several hundred miles off the coast of Chile. All he had was some clothing and bedding, a few tools, a musket, tobacco, and a Bible. He thought he would be rescued by another ship quickly. But months went by.

Selkirk made the best of things. He tamed some wild goats for food and milk and used their skins for clothing. He also had hundreds of cats for company and to keep the rats away. Unlike Robinson Crusoe, he never had another person with him, but he did read his Bible a lot.

After several years, he saw two ships. He soon realized that they were from Spain. England and Scotland had been at war with Spain. Some sailors came ashore and tried to find him. He realized they would probably torture and kill him if he was caught. He hid in the center of the island until eventually they went away.

In February 1709, two English ships came to the island and he was saved. They told him that his ship had sunk not long after dropping him off. Most of the crew had drowned, and the few survivors were thrown into jail in Peru. Selkirk joined the crew of one of the ships that had rescued him and served for several years before he returned home. His family was astonished to see him. They had given him up for lost. He wrote a book about his adventures, which was published in 1712. But the sea was in his blood. He joined the Royal Navy and took another voyage in 1720. He died of a fever the following year while his ship was off the coast of Africa.

This is a portrait of King George I of England. Because George didn't become king until he was 54, it was probably painted while he was still the elector, or ruler, of the German province of Hanover. He became king because his mother, Sophia, was related to James I, an earlier English king. But he wasn't excited about taking over the English throne. He never learned to speak English well and spent as much time as he could in Germany.

The Royal Academy of Music

As things turned out, Handel didn't have much to worry about. The new king apparently didn't hold a grudge. It appears he quickly forgave Handel for staying so long in London. He even doubled the pension that Queen Anne had given him.

George I, who never really enjoyed being in England, returned to Hanover soon after assuming the throne. Handel accompanied him and took the occasion to visit his family in Halle. There he resumed a friendship with a young man named Johann Christoph Schmidt. Schmidt became Handel's secretary and followed him back to England. Schmidt also had a son with the same name. Both changed their names to John Christopher Smith and remained Handel's friends for the rest of his life.

In 1717 Handel composed one of his most famous works, *Water Music.* It was played for the first time during a boat trip that the king took on the Thames River. The king enjoyed it so much that he asked for it to be replayed several times.

By then the earlier interest for Italian opera had faded in London, so Handel spent several years living in the country at an estate known as Cannons. It was the home of the Duke of Chandos. Handel was employed there as court composer.

However, he soon returned to the public eye. To restore the popularity of Italian opera, the Royal Academy of Music was established in 1719. It would perform in King's Theatre, the most prestigious theater in London.

In 1717, Handel composed his Water Music, *one of his most famous works. King George I and members of his court enjoyed a leisurely dinner while they drifted slowly down the Thames River in a large, elaborately decorated barge. Handel and a small orchestra followed closely in another barge, playing the music that Handel had just composed. The king enjoyed the performance so much that he asked for it to be repeated twice.*

The academy was set up like a modern corporation. Investors bought shares of stock, which provided them with the possibility of making a good return on their money. However, if the academy didn't do well, they wouldn't make anything. They could lose their entire investment.

Handel was appointed as its chief composer and musical director. He traveled to Europe to sign up singers, almost all of whom were from Italy. He also made a quick trip to Halle to visit his relatives. Bach made a special trip there to try to meet him, but he was delayed by illness and arrived just a few days after Handel had left. When Handel returned to London, he began writing operas for the academy to produce. People were amazed at how fast he could write an opera, sometimes needing only a few weeks.

Handel wasn't the only composer for the academy. Filippo Amadei and Giovanni Bononcini were the others, and the three were quite competitive. In 1721 the academy's directors created a contest for the three rivals. Each would compose one act of a composite opera, which was called *Muzio Scevola.* Amadei composed Act 1; Bononcini, Act 2; and Handel, Act 3. Handel won the contest.

At first the academy did well. In 1723 Handel leased a house in London's prestigious Mayfair District, which reflected his sense of his own importance in the cultural life of London. He would live there for the rest of his life. Eventually it would be decorated with many pieces of art, including two paintings by Rembrandt.

During this period he also became the music teacher to the royal princesses, the daughters of George II. In 1727 he became a naturalized British citizen.

In the meantime, the academy was showing signs of strain. Putting on operas has always been expensive, and the academy was

no longer showing a profit. In addition, some prominent English writers were opposed to foreign operas. Their negative reviews helped to reduce the potential audience.

There were other problems as well.

Handel still had the same quick temper that had nearly resulted in his death in Hamburg. According to one story, he hated to listen to instruments being tuned. Orchestra members would have to do that task before leaving the theater the night before. One time a practical joker broke in and detuned all the instruments. When Handel gave the signal to begin the performance the following day, the noise was horrible. Handel became enraged. He stomped on a double bass, a large string instrument. He threw a kettledrum at one of the orchestra members (it missed). The wig he was wearing fell off.

In 1723 his most famous singer, an Italian soprano named Francesca Cuzzoni, refused to sing an aria he had written. He stormed over to her, picked her up, and threatened to throw her out the window. "Madam," he shouted, "I know you are a veritable devil, but I would have you know that I am Beelzebub, chief of the Devils."

Several years later he hired another famous soprano, Faustina Bordoni. Bordoni and Cuzzoni didn't get along. Each woman thought she was the better singer and more important than the other. Things got so bad that they actually got into a fistfight on stage during a performance in 1727. That created a huge scandal. The rest of the season was canceled.

By then the public's interest in Italian opera was beginning to fade. The final straw came in 1728 with the premiere of *The Beggar's Opera.* Written in English by John Gay, it was very different from

the academy's operas and became widely popular. The success of *The Beggar's Opera,* coupled with that of several similar productions, meant even lower attendance for academy productions. The investors were tired of throwing money at a project that didn't seem as if it would ever show a profit.

Handel quickly regrouped. In 1729 he went back to mainland Europe to hire new singers for a second attempt to make the academy successful. He also visited his mother. It would be the final time he would see her, as she would die late the following year. Then he returned to London and started all over again. He would still compose and produce Italian operas, but this time the operas would be funded by selling season subscriptions.

The first few seasons were fairly successful. But once again Handel found himself faced with a duel. This one involved much more than swords or a couple of musical instruments. It was between two rival opera companies.

A scene from The Beggar's Opera *by John Gay. Written in English, it was totally different from the Italian operas that Handel composed and became a huge success. This is an engraving by the famous English artist William Hogarth.*

A new group called the Opera of the Nobility took over King's Theatre in 1734. Handel and his group had to move to the nearby Covent Garden Theatre.

The conflict did not affect Handel's creative abilities. In 1734 and 1735 he wrote two of his greatest operas, *Ariodante* and *Alcina.*

However, the eventual outcome of the opera duel was practically inevitable. If one opera company was having problems surviving because the public was losing interest, there was no way there be enough of an audience for two. By 1737, both companies were forced to fold. Even though he was composing other music, Handel's main source of income had disappeared.

As he had done a quarter century earlier, when the elector of Hanover became the king of England, Handel worried about his future. This time, however, he was not a young man with boundless energy. Now he was in his early fifties. Not surprisingly, his health was affected. His right hand became paralyzed. He traveled to a health spa in continental Europe, seeking a cure, but was little relieved.

His job situation was similar to that faced by many people today, people who have spent their entire lives working in an occupation that is suddenly no longer necessary. Many are downsized and struggle to find another job.

Handel struggled, too. When he finally found a position, his new "job" would make him immortal.

EARLY STOCK MARKET CRAZE

FYInfo

Would you give your money to a man who told you that he was forming "a company for carrying on an undertaking of great advantage, but nobody is to know what it is"?

You probably wouldn't. But more than 1,000 Englishmen did in 1720, at the height of a stock market craze that would become known as the South Sea Bubble.

It began in 1711 when the South Sea Company was formed in London. South Sea had been given a monopoly on trading with several countries in Spanish America. Its directors claimed that it would eventually become very profitable. Even though it wasn't making much money, many people were eager to become stockholders. Handel was one of those who believed the directors. He invested 500 pounds (a unit of English money) in 1716, a substantial sum at that time.

In 1720 the craze reached its peak. The stock price soared from 100 pounds in February to 1000 pounds in August. During that time, a number of other newly created companies took advantage of the greed and hysteria that the South Sea Bubble had started. Trading human hair, importing walnut trees from Virginia, and making iron from coal were just a few of the schemes that also attracted investors' money.

And then there was that man who wouldn't tell anybody about his new company. He promised investors that they would all make enough money in the first year alone to cover their initial investment. He didn't ask for all the money up front—just a small deposit. He promised that he'd reveal all the details within a month. When he opened an office one morning, a long line of people was waiting to sign up. He made 2,000 pounds before he closed five hours later. But no one ever found out what his "company" would do. He skipped town that same night and disappeared across the English Channel.

He was one of the lucky ones.

By August, people began to worry about the safety of their investments in the South Sea Company. The value of the stock quickly began to fall, and it dragged down all the other new companies with it. Thousands of people were ruined when their stock—much of it purchased at absurdly high prices—became worthless.

This is perhaps the most famous portrait of Handel. It was painted in 1749 when Handel was at the peak of his fame and prestige. The artist is the English painter Thomas Hudson, who lived between 1701 and 1779.

Messiah

Handel was a supremely practical man. If the public wasn't interested in operas sung in Italian, he would find something else to market. The solution quickly came to him: oratorios sung in English.

An oratorio differs in several ways from an opera. Rather than elaborately costumed singers acting out their parts on stage, oratorio singers wear normal clothes. Most are in the chorus, which is more important in an oratorio than it is in an opera. The solo singers sit in chairs in front of the chorus, rising only when it is their turn to sing. The themes usually come from the Bible, almost always from the Old Testament. Many oratorios deal with people trying to gain their freedom from oppressive rulers, as was the case with the Biblical Jews in Egypt.

Handel had written an oratorio as early as 1732, but at that time he was still putting most of his creative efforts into Italian operas. Now that the public no longer wanted opera, he channeled most of his energy into oratorios. He began in 1738 with *Saul* and *Israel in Egypt*.

Even though he had become famous enough to have a statue resembling him erected in 1738—a remarkable honor for a man who

was still alive—he was having plenty of difficulties. The oratorios hadn't gained the former popularity of the operas. He also found himself the target of frequent criticisms. Many people made fun of him because he spoke broken English with a heavy German accent. Some ridiculed him because of his size: He was large, heavy, and sometimes clumsy. Still others were simply jealous of his fame.

In late 1741 Handel accepted an invitation to go to Dublin, Ireland. To repay his hosts, he gave "that generous and polite nation something new."

The "something new" was *Messiah.*

Set to an arrangement of passages taken from the Bible by a man named Charles Jennens, Handel composed the music while he was still in London, just before his departure for Dublin. It took him just over three weeks. That seems like a short period to create something that has endured for so long, but Handel was used to composing in short bursts of inspiration.

"I did think I did see all Heaven before me and the great God Himself," Handel is believed to have said during the time that he composed *Messiah.*

Knowing the value of promoting his work, he made sure that all the leading newspapers in Dublin were aware of *Messiah*'s upcoming debut on April 13, 1742. One paper, even before the first performance, wrote that it was "the finest Composition of Musick that was ever heard."

Notices issued before the performance asked women "not to come with Hoops this day, as it will greatly increase the Charity, by making Room for more Company," and "the Gentlemen are desired to come without their Swords." Not surprisingly, the premiere was packed. It was a sensation.

One of the singers was Susanna Maria Cibber, a famous London actress who had become involved in a very messy scandal. She had been forced to leave London and go to Dublin. When she sang the aria "He Was Despised," one of the men in the audience called out, "Woman, for this be all thy sins forgiven thee!"

Surprisingly, it wasn't as well-received in London when it premiered there the following year. Just before the performance, one newspaper wrote that it was "profane" and "blasphemous" to perform an oratorio that used sacred words for "diversion and amusement." Perhaps with Ms. Cibber in mind, the paper also criticized the singers as "a Set of People very unfit to perform so solemn a Service."

Jennens himself wasn't impressed. In several letters to a friend, he complained, "*Messiah* has disappointed me, being set in great hast, tho' he said he would be a year about it, & make it the best of all his Compositions. I shall put no more Sacred Works into his hands, to be thus abus'd. . . . 'tis still in his power by retouching the weak parts to make it fit for a publick performance; & I have said a great deal to him on the Subject; but he is so lazy and so obstinate, that I much doubt the Effect."

Jennens concluded by saying Handel "has made a fine Entertainment of it, tho' not near so good as he might & ought to have done." Future generations would profoundly disagree with that judgment.

At least one person at the London premiere was impressed. When King George II heard the Hallelujah Chorus, he rose to his feet. Ever since, it has been customary for audiences to stand as the first notes of the Hallelujah Chorus ring out, remain standing while it is being sung, then resume their seats as the final chords echo through the hall.

No other piece of music has commanded that respect. Handel reportedly said about his work, "Whether I was in my body or out of my body as I wrote it I know not. God knows."

The words of the Hallelujah Chorus come from three selections from the Book of Revelation at the end of the New Testament: *"Hallelujah: for the Lord God Omnipotent reigneth* (Revelation 19:6). *The kingdom of this world/is become the kingdom of our Lord,/and of his Christ;/and He shall reign for ever and ever* (Revelation 11:15). *King of Kings, and Lord of Lords* (Revelation 19:16). *Hallelujah!*

Just thirty-nine words, sung over and over again in less than four minutes. Yet it is hard to think of another piece of music that has endured so long with so much affection attached to it.

Handel would likely be surprised that we consider *Messiah* as Christmas music. Even though nearly all of its performances today occur during the Christmas season, it is no accident that its premiere occurred during the Easter season. Jennens viewed it as music for Passion Week—the weeklong holiday commemorating the period between the entrance of Jesus into Jerusalem and the Resurrection.

Only the first part of *Messiah* deals directly with Christmas and the birth of Jesus. The second—and longest—part, which concludes with the magnificent Hallelujah Chorus, deals with Christ's crucifixion. According to the Christian religion, that represents his sacrifice for the human race. The third section, by far the shortest, reveals the Christian soul's victory over death.

Certainly *Messiah* reveals the victory of Handel's reputation over death. He would be counted among the world's greatest composers on the basis of *Messiah* alone.

But at the time it was not much more than just another of his hundreds of compositions. He still had to make a living.

How a German Prince Became King of England

FYInfo

When George II stood during the Hallelujah Chorus at the London premiere of *Messiah* in 1743, it marked an unusual moment. The king of England, who was born in Germany, was honoring England's most famous composer—also born in Germany. How did a German prince become king of England?

The answer starts with Queen Elizabeth I, who died in 1603 without leaving an heir after ruling England for forty-five years. Many years previously her aunt Mary, the sister of her father, King Henry VIII, married James IV, the king of Scotland. At that time, England and Scotland were separate countries. James and Mary had a son who ruled Scotland as James V. He in turn had a daughter, who became known as Mary, Queen of Scots. Her son—James VI of Scotland—became James I of England in 1603 because he had the best claim to the English throne when Elizabeth died.

On James's death in 1625, his son became king as Charles I. But Charles quarreled with the English Parliament. That led to a long civil war that Charles and his supporters eventually lost. Charles was beheaded in 1649. The leader of the Parliament troops, Oliver Cromwell, became head of the government. Cromwell died in 1658.

After two years of political instability, Charles's son, Charles II, was installed as the English king in 1660. Many people were glad to have a king again. Charles II died in 1685 without leaving any direct heirs.

His younger brother became King James II. But James quickly became very unpopular. As a result, many important statesmen in England invited William of Orange (a Dutch province) to take over the throne. William, who was married to James's daughter Mary, easily brushed his father-in-law aside.

Mary died in 1694 and William followed eight years later. They had no children. Mary's younger sister Anne became queen in 1702. She didn't have any children either, and she died in 1714.

According to the Act of Succession, passed in 1701, the next in line was Sophia. Like Charles II and James II, she was a granddaughter of James I. She married Ernest Augustus, the elector, or ruler, of the German province of Hanover. Sophia died two months before Queen Anne. Her son became George I of England in 1714 at the age of fifty-four.

He wasn't entirely happy about being the English king. He didn't make much effort to learn how to speak English. He also spent as much time in Hanover as he could. When he died in 1727, his son—who had been born in Hanover in 1683—became George II. He ruled until his death in 1760, the year after Handel died.

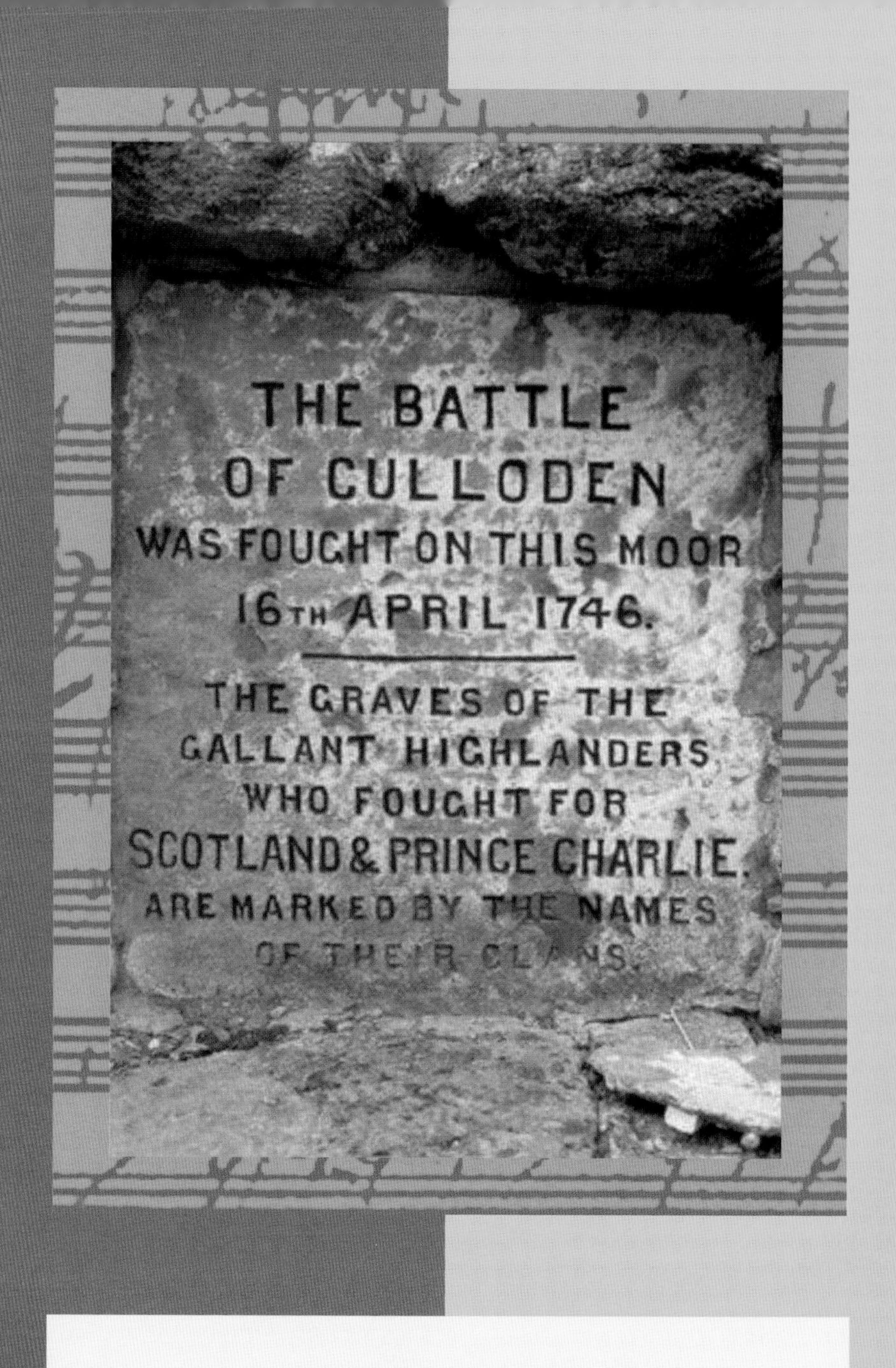

This stone is at the site of the Battle of Culloden, located in northern Scotland near the town of Inverness. "Bonnie Prince Charlie," who had a claim to the English throne, raised an army and invaded England in 1745. After some successes, he retreated to Scotland and was defeated the following year.

The Peak of Popularity

Handel achieved the height of his fame during the years following *Messiah.* He composed many more oratorios, which included *Belshazzar, Semele,* and *Joseph and His Brethren.* The most famous at the time—far eclipsing *Messiah*—was *Judas Maccabaeus.* It was based on the story of one of the last great Jewish leaders prior to the birth of Jesus. It had a very contemporary appeal as well.

For years, many people, especially those in Scotland, had been opposed to George II. An army under the leadership of "Bonnie Prince Charlie," a descendant of the deposed James II through his second marriage, invaded England in 1745. Their objective was to reestablish the type of monarchy that would reduce the power of the people. At the Battle of Culloden in 1746, the invaders were defeated.

When *Judas Maccabaeus* debuted the following year, everyone knew that it was a celebration of the English victory. Its most famous chorus, "See, the Conquering Hero Comes," is a very stirring piece of music. It is often played today.

The success of *Judas Maccabaeus* was important financially also. After several years of barely breaking even, Handel finally saw clear

profit for a season of music. This piece of music would be performed more than fifty times during his lifetime.

In 1749 Handel wrote another famous piece, *Royal Fireworks Music.* It features a large wind section including trumpets and French horns. It was so popular that 12,000 people attended a rehearsal. The turnout created a traffic jam that blocked London Bridge for three hours. In an early instance of road rage, several people were injured during fights while they waited for normal traffic to get under way again.

The following year Handel journeyed to Germany. It would be the last time that he set foot in his native land. In a coach accident in The Netherlands, he was hurt but made a quick recovery. But when he returned to England and began work on what would be his final oratorio, *Jephtha,* he began having health problems from which he would not recover.

On February 13, 1751, he wrote that he was "unable to go on owing to weakening of the sight of my left eye."

By the time of *Jephtha*'s premiere one year later, he had gone completely blind in one eye; six months later he lost the sight in his other eye. He tried several painful operations, but nothing worked.

A 1753 performance of *Messiah* is the last known instance of Handel's performing in public. By then, *Messiah* was being performed several times every year—always in the spring, and almost always to benefit one of his favorite charities, the Foundling Hospital, a home for orphans.

Although he'd lost his sight, he didn't lose his sense of humor. Samuel Sharp, his eye surgeon, asked his patient if he would continue to play the organ at performances of his oratorios.

"No," Handel replied.

Sharp recommended a famous blind organist and performer named John Stanley as a possible replacement. "His memory never fails," Sharp added.

Handel began laughing. "Mr. Sharp, have you never read the Scriptures?" he asked. "Do you not remember, if the blind lead the blind, they will both fall in the ditch?"

The following year, his opera *Admeto, re di Tessaglia* was performed. It would be the last time that any opera of Handel's would be produced for well over 150 years.

Although it was difficult, Handel continued to compose. His final major work, *The Triumph of Time and Truth,* made its debut on March 11, 1757. The younger John Christopher Smith helped out at many productions of Handel's works during the final years, often serving as conductor.

After attending a performance of *Messiah* on April 6, 1759, Handel complained of faintness and was confined to his bed. He would never emerge.

On the night of April 13, a friend named James Smyth visited him. Smyth wrote, "At 7 o'clock in the evening he took leave of me, and told me we 'should meet again.' As soon as I was gone he told his servant '*not* to let me come to him any more, for that he had now done with this world.' He died as he lived—a good *Christian,* with true sense of his duty to God and man, and in perfect charity with all the world."

George Frideric Handel died early the following morning. His fame was so great that his burial six days later at Westminster Abbey, where many of the great men of England are buried, attracted more than 3,000 mourners. One newspaper wrote, "There was almost the greatest Concourse of People of all Ranks ever seen upon such, or indeed upon any other occasion."

In 1762, according to his wishes, a monument was erected by his burial site. It depicts the composer holding the score of *Messiah.* The score is opened to the music for "I Know That My Redeemer Liveth."

Many other composers thought very highly of Handel.

"Handel is the greatest composer who ever lived. I would bare my head and kneel at his grave," said Ludwig van Beethoven a few years before his own death.

When he heard the Hallelujah Chorus for the first time, Austrian composer Joseph Haydn exclaimed, "He is the master of us all!"

Not everyone was as impressed. Russian composer Peter Tchaikovsky sneered, "Handel is only fourth rate. He is not even interesting." And French composer Hector Berlioz added that he was "a tub of pork and beer."

But most people, whether they are composers, musical experts, or those who simply enjoy music, would disagree with such comments. Handel seems destined to remain one of the most famous composers of classical music who ever lived.

Charles Burney, who knew him well, wrote, "The figure of Handel was large, and he was somewhat corpulent, and unwieldy in his motion. He was impetuous, rough, and peremptory in his manners and conversations, but totally devoid of ill-nature or malevolence. His general look was somewhat heavy and sour; but when he did smile, it was his sire the sun, bursting out of a black cloud. There was a sudden flash of intelligence, wit, and good humor, beaming in his countenance, which I hardly saw in any other."

It is appropriate that *Messiah* was the final music that Handel ever heard, for through it Handel has enriched the lives of countless millions of people down through the centuries.

HALLEY'S COMET

FYInfo

Handel's blindness would likely have prevented him from observing firsthand one of the astronomical marvels of his time: the return in late 1758 of what had just become known as Halley's comet.

What made its sight in the sky night after night even more spectacular was that it showed up exactly on schedule.

In 1705 Edmond Halley, who had already established a reputation in astronomy and several other fields, announced that a comet which he had observed in 1682 was actually the same one that had been widely reported in 1456, 1531, and 1607. It was also the same comet that had appeared over England in the year 1066, when the Normans from France had invaded England and conquered it. On the basis of a series of complex mathematical calculations, he predicted that it would return in 53 more years. When it appeared during the Christmas season of 1758, exactly when Halley predicted it would, it was quickly named in his honor.

Halley was born in 1656 in the village of Haggerston, which is now part of London. His father was a well-to-do merchant, and the boy received a good education at the prestigious St. Paul's School. In 1671, at the age of fifteen, he was appointed school captain, a position similar to being student body president today.

Halley entered Oxford University in 1673. There he met John Flamsteed, the Royal Astronomer. Flamsteed had compiled a catalog of the stars visible from the northern hemisphere. Inspired by Flamsteed, Halley sailed to tiny St. Helena Island, located in the middle of the South Atlantic Ocean. He wanted to make a catalog like Flamsteed's for southern hemisphere stars.

During his year on the remote island, Halley charted more than 300 stars. For his work, he was named as a member of the prestigious Royal Academy at the young age of twenty-two. During a long scientific career that followed, he also studied weather patterns, the earth's magnetic field, and ocean tides. He calculated a way of watching the passage of the planet Venus across the sun's disk that helped to accurately measure the distance between Earth and the sun. He succeeded Flamsteed as Royal Astronomer in 1720. He died in 1742, long before the reappearance of the comet.

Selected Works

Oratorios
Saul
Israel in Egypt
Messiah
Samson
Judas Maccabaeus
Jephtha
Joseph and His Brethren
Joshua
Solomon
Alceste

Operas
Ariodante
Alcina
Giulio Cesare
Tamerlano

Orchestral Works
Royal Fireworks Music
Water Music
Organ Concertos
Concerti Grossi

Other Vocal Works
Ode for St. Cecilia's Day
Coronation Anthems

Chronology

1685 Georg Friedrich Händel born on February 23
1697 father dies
1702 enters University of Halle, then is named church organist
1703 leaves Halle for Hamburg
1704 duels with Johann Mattheson
1705 premiere of first opera, *Almira*
1706 travels to Italy
1710 accepts job as kapellmeister to Georg Ludwig, elector of Hanover, then travels to England for the first time
1712 travels to England again
1717 composes *Water Music*
1719 as chief composer and musical director, forms Royal Academy of Music
1727 becomes English citizen
1730 mother dies
1738 composes *Saul,* his first major oratorio in English
1741 composes *Messiah*
1742 *Messiah* premieres in Dublin, Ireland, on April 13
1746 composes *Judas Maccabaeus,* which premieres the following year
1749 composes *Royal Fireworks Music*
1751 blindness sets in, complete by the following year
1757 composes *The Triumph of Time and Truth,* his final major work
1759 dies on April 14

Timeline in History

1517	Martin Luther nails his 95 Theses to cathedral door, setting in motion events that become known as the Protestant Reformation
1607	first English settlement in the New World is established at Jamestown, Virginia
1677	ice cream becomes popular as dessert in Paris, France
1681	dodo, a flightless bird, becomes extinct
1685	birth of Johann Sebastian Bach less than one month after Handel is born
1689	Peter the Great becomes czar of Russia; William and Mary become king and queen of England, Ireland, and Scotland
1692	Salem witch trials
1706	birth of Benjamin Franklin
1707	Scotland and England unite as Great Britain
1709	invention of piano
1712	last execution for witchcraft in England
1714	George I becomes English king
1719	Daniel Defoe publishes *Robinson Crusoe*
1720	South Sea Bubble, England's first great stock market crash
1726	Jonathan Swift publishes *Gulliver's Travels*
1727	George II becomes English king
1732	birth of George Washington
1735	birth of Paul Revere and John Adams, who becomes second U.S. president
1743	birth of Thomas Jefferson, who writes Declaration of Independence and becomes third U.S. President
1756	birth of Wolfgang Amadeus Mozart
1765	James Watt invents the steam engine
1770	birth of Ludwig van Beethoven
1776	Declaration of Independence signed by thirteen American colonies

Further Reading

For Young Adults

Anderson, M. T. *Handel: Who Knew What He Liked.* Cambridge, Mass.: Candlewick Press, 2001.

Hammond, Susan. *Hallelujah Handel* (Audio CD). Chicago: Children's Bookstore, 1995.

Handel, George Frideric. Illustrated by Barry Moser. *Messiah: The Wordbook for the Oratorio.* New York: HarperCollins, 1992.

Ludwig, Charles. *George Frideric Handel, Composer of* Messiah. Milford, Mich.: Mott Media, 1987.

Wheeler, Opal. *Handel at the Court of Kings.* New York: E.P. Dutton, 1943.

Works Consulted

Burrows, Donald. *Handel.* Oxford University Press, 2000.

Burrows, Donald, ed. *The Cambridge Companion to Handel.* Cambridge University Press, 1997.

Dean, Winton. *The New Grove Handel.* New York: W.W. Norton, 1982.

Hogwood, Christopher. *Handel.* Bath, England: Thames and Hudson, 1984.

Keates, Jonathan. *Handel: The Man and His Music.* London: Victor Gollancz Ltd., 1985.

LaRue, C. Steven. *Handel and his Singers.* Oxford: Clarendon Press, 1995.

Luckett, Richard. *Handel's Messiah—A Celebration.* New York: Harcourt Brace, 1992.

Rackwitz, Werner, and Helmut Steffens. *George Frideric Handel: A Biography in Pictures.* Leipzig, Germany: VEB Deutscher Verlag, 1964.

Schonberg, Harold C. *The Lives of the Great Composers.* New York: W.W. Norton, 1981.

Thompson, Wendy. *Handel.* New York: Omnibus Press, 1994.

On the Internet

Bibliography/Catalog of Compositions: http://www.GFHandel.org

Picture Gallery, List of Works: http://w3.rz-berlin.mpg.de/cmp/handel.html

Bio from the Internet Public Library: http://www.ipl.org/div/mushist/bar/handel.htm

Detailed biography by period: http://www.amarcordes.ch/compositeurs/haendel_grove.htm

Note to Researchers

The main contemporary source of information about Handel comes from a biography written by the Reverend John Mainwaring, published in 1760, the year after Handel's death. It was the first biography ever written about a musician. Mainwaring never knew Handel, but got much of his information from Handel's secretary, John Christopher Smith; the book is full of inaccuracies. Handel was very secretive about himself and large gaps exist in the Handel chronology. We know almost nothing about his private life. However, over the years, information has been reconstructed about Handel, put together from bits and pieces left to us by people who knew him.

Glossary

amours (ah-MOOR)—love affairs.

aria (AHR-ee-ah)—vocal piece for a single singer, accompanied by orchestra.

Baroque (bah-ROKE)—type of art characterized by complex forms, a great deal of ornaments, and the use of contrasting elements (such as loud and soft musical tones) to produce drama.

blasphemous (BLAS-feh-mes)—showing disrespect for God.

clavichord (KLAH-vih-kord)—earliest keyboard instrument, which uses strings to produce sounds.

deposed (dee-POZED)—removed from the throne.

elector (ee-LEK-tor)—ruler of a German province.

harpsichord (HARP-si-kord)—keyboard instrument in which the strings are plucked.

impetuous (im-PET-chew-us)—inclined to act in a rash or hurried manner without thought of the consequences.

kapellmeister (keh-PELL-my-ster)—leader of an orchestra at the court of a nobleman.

malevolence (meh-LEH-vol-ents)—intending to do or cause evil.

opera (AW-prah)—costumed dramatic performance set to music, which includes soloists, chorus, and orchestra.

oratorio (or-ah-TOR-ee-oh)—large-scale musical composition for orchestra, chorus, and soloists, usually based on a religious theme.

ornate (or-NATE)—fancily decorated.

parried (PAH-reed)—turned aside.

peremptory (per-EMP-teh-ree)—very self-assured; not allowing disagreement.

profane (proh-FANE)—demonstrating disrespect for sacred things.

soprano (seh-PRAH-noh)—the highest voice range.

Index